7-Day

Brain Power Challenge

7-Day

BRAIN POWER

CHALLENGE

Increase Brain Power In 7 Days

CHALLENGE SELF

http://www.ChallengeSelf.com

Challenging Publishing

ISBN 978-1-537-15698-9

Printed in the United States of America

First Edition

YOUR OVERVIEW:

Your Instructions:

How to Best Approach This

This book is not meant to be read entirely in one sitting, but for over the span of each day.

Why? The reasons are relatively simple. We do want you to benefit from the information, which will take time to process, and we do not want to overwhelm you with all the applications of what you will learn. At the same time, we don't want to make this another breezy one-time read, and then you're off to do something else, forgetting your new knowledge without ever applying it to anything.

Now you probably will be eager and tempted to go through this all in one sitting, but we're encouraging you to take it slow. Remember that the best way to approach this is <u>one day</u> at a time. Do not move on to the next day until you have completed its previous day(s).

This approach is effective because if you truly want to improve, you need to remain grounded in the process. There is no such thing as a magic pill; there is continuous conditioned improvement. Rome wasn't built in a day. Likewise, none of the top performers, best athletes, and successful people in the world have gotten to where they are in a day. Breaking things up into separate days supports an ongoing process and builds upon each previous day's progress to bring it all home in the end.

Of course, each individual's experience will be different. You may or may not accomplish your goal after the entire trial is over. In that case, you can repeat it all again starting from Day 1 to the last day.

If you commit yourself, you will see improvement. Are you ready to proceed on to your challenges? Then let's begin!

P.S. If you ever need to contact us, you can always reach out to us at our official website:

http://www.ChallengeSelf.com

Your Challenge:

Train Your Brain

An Organic Superhuman Computer

The human brain is a pretty remarkable creation. Quite possibly, it is the closest nature has ever come to building what is, basically, an organic super computer.

Through an intertwining network of neurons and synapses, it's a multifaceted biological mechanism that performs a variety of functions all at once. The brain is where all of the commands for bodily functions, memories, thoughts, and dreams are stored. Truly, it's an incredible meat machine.

However, like all machines, its ability to function properly begins to *degrade* over time. Sadly, this deterioration affects even the best and brightest of us. In time, people's brain power slows in such a way that memory is no longer as sharp as it once was and the ability to work longer hours and generate brilliant ideas becomes more difficult as well. Such an inevitability of the brain's descent would appear to be something we all have to accept as a fact of life.

But wait, there's hope! The **good news** is that it is possible to preserve your brain's ability to stay healthy and active for much longer than ever before. The best methods to date include mind-stimulating techniques and maintaining a healthy lifestyle. Making the most of a combination of these is a way of unlocking your potential by enhancing your **brain power.**

With enhanced brain power, you'll start to notice an increased concentration on a variety of things including work, school, home life, or just about anything you put your mind to! With a sharper and more concise memory, you'll begin to feel more alert and lucid as your enthusiasm to take in the world around you is stimulated and amplified.

Before proceeding any further, ask yourself this: "Do I fall into the category of feeling like my mind is in the process of becoming mush and sluggish to the point where I'm beginning to suffer from memory loss, or find it difficult to focus on tasks?"

If you answered "yes," then a **seven-day brain training** is just what you need to get your mind back on track! Since the computing power of the brain is like a muscle, you will find that you will need to "work out" with it in order to make the most use of it. A brain power program is an excellent method for doing just that.

Once you're ready to start the seven-day brain power program, there are a few things to consider for a healthy brain that functions well within its capacities.

Some Foods for Thought

Healthy nutrition is an important factor to consider when speeding up your brain. This also includes adjusting to a healthy lifestyle as well.

Below is a brief guide that provides some of the best suggestions for a diet that promotes a healthy brain. Also included are some strategies to promote brain power.

The list provided, while nowhere close to exhaustive, does include some of the most commonly accessible items available that you can try adding to your diet throughout the week to empower your mind and body.

Foods that help to promote a healthy brain include:

Whole Grains: They can be found in cereals, granary bread, rice, and pasta, and are an excellent way to bring energy to the brain. Doing so helps you concentrate and focus on tasks throughout the day. Whole grains with a low GI are very useful here, especially when it comes to those with diabetic concerns.

Oily Fish: It's funny to think about how many of us were told as kids that eating more fish would make us smarter. As it turns out, this is more than an old wives' tale and it's actually been scientifically proven that certain properties in fish can have a positive effect on the brain. What's critical to consider here is how important fats are for healthy brain functions. To get these, it's best to eat fish like salmon, trout, mackerel, sardines, and pilchards as well as flaxseed, soya beans, pumpkin seeds, and walnuts.

Blueberries: Studies conducted at Tuft University and by scientists like Barbara Shukitt-Hale, Ph.D., of Tufts' HNRCA Neuroscience and Aging Laboratory showed a correlation between the consumption of blueberries and a delay in short-term memory loss. In other words, by indulging in this delicious berry via smoothies, cereals, or with snacks like antioxidant-enriched dark chocolate, you can strengthen the power of your memory.

Tomatoes: On the subject of antioxidants, tomatoes contain a healthy helping of lycopene. This amazing phytochemical compound can help protect the brain against the kind of free-radical cell degradation that often leads to dementia. So, this means more meals containing the reddest, juiciest tomatoes you can find. Slice them or dice them and toss them on a salad or a taco, or just snack on them all on their own throughout your day.

B vitamins and folic acids: Found in leafy green vegetables such as spinach and asparagus, they can reduce levels of the dreaded homocysteine, a compound in the blood responsible for cognitive impairment and Alzheimer.

Black currant berries: Rich in vitamin C, these spicy berries can help increase mental sharpness and can help fight the age-related effects of dementia and Alzheimer.

Pumpkin seeds: These seeds contain a key ingredient for enhancing memory and cognitive capacities—zinc.

Broccoli: This easily accessible vegetable contains vitamin K, which is not only known to increase brain function, but also helps with blood clotting as well.

Nuts: Rich in vitamin E, this vast variety (as seen in sweet, spicy, and salty snack mixes galore) can help to prevent the brain from slowing down by stalling the effects of cognitive decline.

Alternative Supple-MENTAL Boosts

There's a plethora of natural alternatives and remedies one can find that help to improve memory and brain functions.

Typically, they to come in the form of teas or herbal infusions.

With many of them originating from Asia, they also have a tendency to be very exotic and have strange names. But their foreign nature shouldn't be alarming or off-putting.

In this case, one should embrace the strange. Especially since studies show, like one conducted at the University of Northumbria in Newcastle, England presented to the annual 2016 British Psychological Society Conference in Nottingham, how, when certain herbs are prepared via an infusion, they can be beneficial to one's brain functions.

Some of the herbal mental amplifiers include:

Gingko Biloba: Possessing an almost mystical quality, this herb has been used in traditional Chinese medicine and has demonstrated a range of benefits. Some of these include increased blood flow to the brain (a must for intensified thinking skills) and an accelerated memory to help fight dementia.

Matcha: Great news for the green tea addicts! This one from Japan has a potency so great that it's alleged to be as powerful as ten cups of regular green tea. The magnitude of effects it has on the tea connoisseur includes increased concentration and a better mood.

Periwinkle and Ginseng: Familiar names to most who are in know about herbs, these two work well together as an infusion drink as they can improve cognitions.

Gotu Kola: Another herb that has its origins in Asia, it's said to boost brain power and contain adaptogenic qualities that have a calming effect on the user, thus reducing stress.

All of these herbal alternatives above are very effective at helping to activate the brain and enhance its functions. However, as a general rule of thumb, it can be said that

green teas (most anyway) have properties that help calm the body and speed up the brain. A key ingredient that helps out a lot with this is **theanine**, an amino acid that increases alpha wave activity.

Something really great to appreciate about these herbal remedies is that they're non-addictive, so there's no dependency or feeling like a zombie when you realize it's time to go back to the market to get some more.

Taken daily, they'll help you focus and make your brain more alert. So, go out and buy some (in their most natural form, as grounded leaves, of course) for this seven-day brain-empowering experiment.

Lifestyle Choices Matter

Your brain is a part of you—and how you go about your everyday life does affect it.

We all know that we're supposed to get the recommended seven to eight hours of sleep, but studies show that it might be helpful to add a little more time to the alarm. According to a study conducted by a Dr. Jessica Payne, a cognitive neuroscientist and assistant professor at the University of Notre Dame, adding twenty more minutes to the clock at bedtime can help boost productivity and performance in the workplace by one hundred percent or more.

Also, it turns out, what's good for the body is also great for the brain—exercise more! Makes sense seeing as there's bundles upon bundles of nervous system webbing that connects the two! Specialists agree. For instance, Nicola Gates, a clinical neuropsychologist at the University of New South Wales Center for Healthy Brain Ageing, suggests that aerobic activity combined with resistance and flexibility training have shown to have brain-boosting effects. Thus, the more active the heart is, the more blood flow reaches the brain, hence a stronger mind.

So, if you're really determined to have a more effective mind and are ready to power up your brain, it's high time to bite the bullet and just make the necessary adjustments to your lifestyle.

You'll be thanking yourself later for this!

Real-Life Smart Drugs

For most people, the very idea of memory-enhancing drugs is a totally *alien concept*.

In fact, someone talking about them at work might be hit with a urine test due to simple ignorance on the part of their employers and colleagues. Likewise, talking about this with friends might have them thinking you're discussing something illegal or some magical substance fabricated for a big Hollywood production. (Think Bradley Cooper in *Limitless*.)

The verdict has been reached: they are more than a fantasy and totally legal. Called **nootropics**, these are often referred to as cognition enhancers or "smart drugs." Usually appearing in bottles in the form of supplements, nootropics can help improve your cognitive abilities in variety of areas including memory, creativity, motivation, or executive functions.

Derived from the Greek words *nous* or "mind" and *trepin* or "bend," the term nootropic was first coined by Romanian Psychologist Corneliu E. Giurgea in 1972 as a way of describing how the properties of these supplements function. The basic idea was that taking these types of drugs would help bend and reshape the mind to function at a *greater capacity*.

Typically, nootropics have been used by students trying to cope with the strains created by the demands of their studies. Some of the more common forms include Amphetamine (widely prescribed as "Adderall" for *attention deficit hyperactivity disorder*), Methylphenidate, Eugeroic (marketed as "modafinil" under the brand Provigil to treat *narcolepsy*), Xanthine (caffeine), and even Nicotine.

More often than not, you need a prescription by a doctor, not only for access, but also with regard to dosage and use. The most obvious concern here is, of course, with regard to side effects. Like any drug, there is a risk of developing a dependency or a risk of going above the prescribed amount.

Thus, it's an absolute imperative to take these supplements responsibly and only after consulting a doctor. That way, you can be safe knowing you have the ones that best meet your mental and physical health needs and to be sure you're taking the right amount of each.

An Important Note

One final note before proceeding forward: you should consult your physician to see if there is a possibility of complications or negative effects stemming from the suggested supplement use. It's also important to note the responsibility for talking to your doctor about any and all health-related concerns related to any of the following activities is entirely at your own discretion.

As a disclaimer, we cannot be held accountable for any possible or unforeseen complications or injuries that may occur due acting upon the advice presented. The information provided is **NOT** intended to act as a substitute for the advice from your doctor or other medical professional.

Now that we have gotten that out of the way, and without further delay, it's time to begin your seven-day brain power challenge!

DAY 1:

Start Rebooting Your Brain

A Sharp Mind Begins with a Clear Head

The practice of **clear thinking** is quite possibly the brain's greatest asset. Being able to interpret and apply reason to the world around us is the most effective way to exist within reality. At its peak, the brain's capacity to function within the parameters of clearer thinking is the best way to work it out—as "a muscle."

One way of approaching the concept of clear thinking via brain stimulation is to think of it as *solving an equation*. With that "in mind," here's a step-by-step process:

STEP 1: *Start early.* Jump starting your brain in the morning before engaging in other activities is the best way to begin. Go ahead and add some of the aforementioned brain power foods into your breakfast as you get started.

STEP 2: *Keep a routine.* It might be tricky in the beginning, but it will get easier as you start to incorporate natural supplements, such as Ginkgo biloba or Matcha green teas, combined with the brain-empowering techniques into your lifestyle to the point that they become second nature. To get the mental juices flowing, initiate your clear thinking by taking **fifteen** to **twenty minutes** out of your morning to fire up those synapses:

In a calm setting, close your eyes, focus on your breathing, and start thinking about **3 clear thoughts** you have at that very instant.

STEP 3: *Analyze your thoughts.* Consider these things that have popped into your mind on an individual basis and take a moment to give some consideration as to why they dominate your thoughts. For example, maybe you're preoccupied by your work or money (or a combination thereof). From there, you could go deeper in asking yourself *why you're thinking* about these things. Or perhaps, consider the way that you are feeling and maybe what the root causes are of the stress that might be aligned with these concerns in your life.

STEP 4: *Answer your own questions.* Doing so during this semi-meditational practice will be like you're stepping out of your own body to greet and converse with your psyche.

This daily mental exercise will help to **keep your mind alert**. Likewise, the more you make it a part of your morning routine, the more it will become a part of your day-to-day habits.

Know Your State of Mind First

By making the practice of clear thinking **your state of mind** throughout the day (and every day that follows), you will start to find aspects of your own thought processes, such as decision-making, become more defined. You will also find yourself having become less distracted and less annoyed by what others throw at you as your delve into the core of your very own thoughts.

For the purposes of this entire process, it's best to view **Day 1** as a kind of warm-up before jumping head-first into the nitty-gritty of this week. Doing so will allow you to gain some insight into what is really going on in your head.

Think of practicing clear thinking as a sort of behind-the-scenes look into what you can expect as you start to notice changes to your thought processes.

On **Day 2,** we'll start to bite down into the meat of your brain training.

DAY 2:

Entrain Your Brain to Create New Neural Pathways

Rhythmic Sensory Stimulation

We all know about the soothing sensation we get when we listen to raindrops falling against our roof or the sound of waves crashing upon a beach. These types of ambient noises have the ability to actually help us relax, encourage positivistic thinking, or to drift off into sleep with ease.

This calming effect stems from the brain's own bio-electric responses to pulses, either from sound or light, also known as "rhythmic sensory stimulation."

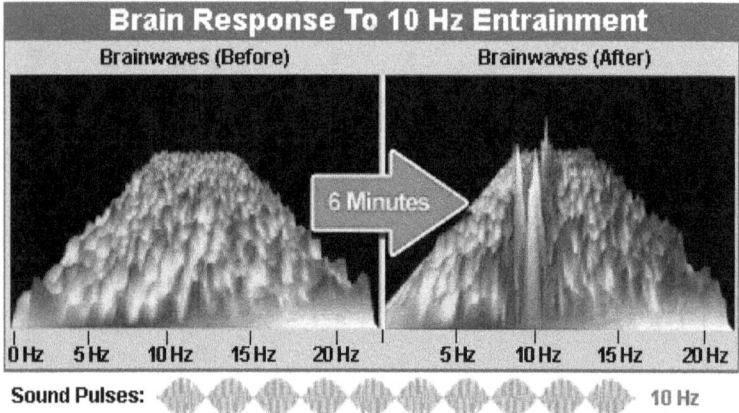

Brain entrainment, on the other hand, has to do with the synchronization of two or more rhythmic cycles. This process can be achieved through the use of light sounds that can actually help stimulate your brain to stay focused by emitting sounds into it directly.

A series of studies conducted, such as by Japanese professor Tsuyoshi Inouye of the Department of Neuropsychiatry at

Osaka University Medical School, helped to establish a link between *rhythmic sensory stimulation* and *cerebral synchronization* when shown under EEG monitoring.

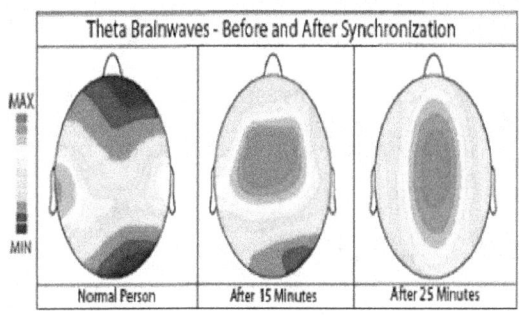

Here's an example of light, ambient sounds that can be used for brain stimulation*:

www.youtube.com/watch?v=5wNkBjuU5jk

*Like nootropics, don't expect miracles at work here. This is real life, not like the movies, but brain entrainment certainly does help with increasing brain activities.

Enhance Brain Functions Manually By Manipulating Your Brainwaves

Also called **binaural beats,** these sounds come in different frequencies that range from high (above 40 HZ) to low (below 4 HZ). Each one corresponds to different wave types that evoke a unique stimulation in the brain.

Frequency Types Include:

Above 40 HZ: Emits *Gamma Waves* that are geared towards problem solving, fear, perception, and consciousness.

Between 39 to 13 HZ: Emits *Beta Waves* that can evoke feelings of active or anxious thinking, concentration, focused cognition, paranoia, or arousal.

Between 13 to 7 HZ: Emits *Alpha Waves* that promote relaxation and dreams during sleep.

Between 7 to 4 HZ: Emits *Theta Waves* that can be used for deep meditation and relaxation.

Lower than 4 HZ: Emits *Delta Waves* that can be used for dreamless sleep and a loss of body awareness.

BrainWaves Graph

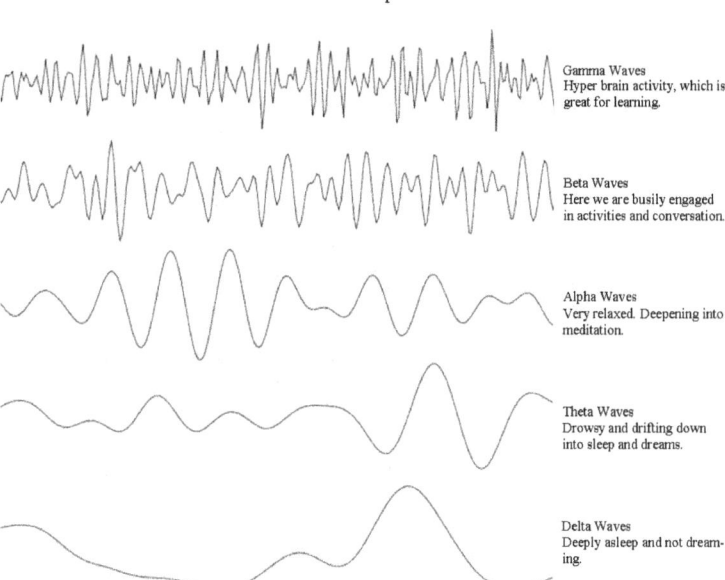

Gamma Waves
Hyper brain activity, which is great for learning.

Beta Waves
Here we are busily engaged in activities and conversation.

Alpha Waves
Very relaxed. Deepening into meditation.

Theta Waves
Drowsy and drifting down into sleep and dreams.

Delta Waves
Deeply asleep and not dreaming.

Throughout this week, these different frequencies will be used to give you more brain power in the various areas of stimulation.

To make things a little easier for you, here's the <u>binaural beat playlist</u>* you can use for the week.

*Now please note we are not in any way affiliated with them and do not claim nor guarantee any results. Feel to use other binaural beats that stimulate the specific brainwaves.

These sounds are anything but typical and may be harsh for some folks to tolerate at first, and may need some *getting used to*. That's why we've provided <u>two versions</u>: **meditation** and **raw**.

The *meditation version* is softer for a more pleasant listening sound while the *raw version* will be more effective because you're getting the binaural sound without the music layer on top of the sound. (Think of the former as eating *chocolate-coated broccoli* and the latter *raw broccoli*. Do you prefer tastier or healthier?)

Gamma Waves

- Meditation Version:

www.youtube.com/watch?v=clwVxrQ3vFo

- Raw Version:

www.youtube.com/watch?v=axTImghP9Ts

Beta Waves

- Meditation Version:

www.youtube.com/watch?v=z-tf5Iu5io8

- Raw Version:

www.youtube.com/watch?v=vEHVz5XCmBs

Alpha Waves

- Meditation Version:

www.youtube.com/watch?v=27cv2zHRkIE

- Raw Version:

www.youtube.com/watch?v=7cHjaJRl1Qo

Theta Waves
- Meditation Version:

www.youtube.com/watch?v=CreU9g302yU

- Raw Version:

www.youtube.com/watch?v=66tq9xji0xA

Delta Waves
- Meditation Version:

www.youtube.com/watch?v=txQ6t4yPIM0

- Raw Version:

www.youtube.com/watch?v=JnhFsHyeeNQ

Note: Some of these frequency videos run for about an hour, but it isn't necessary to sit through the whole track to benefit from the effect. Just play an individual track when you need to focus during a particular activity in your day or night, and simply stop when you're finished.

Exercise: The Brain Entrainment Session

STEP 1: **Day 2** starts with your brain-boosting breakfast. At this point, it's not important to include the supplements just yet, but feel free to include your regular morning joe or cup of tea.

STEP 2: *Download/Save** one of the frequency links to your phone or other device and give it a listen. They are to be listened to with headphones.

*It's not necessary to download all of the links (unless you really want to, of course). Instead, pick one whose description of mind effects best meets what you want to accomplish for the day. For example, if you have some tasks at hand that will require a greater degree of *mental activity* for the day, then it would be best to select the **Gamma Waves** track. By contrast, if *wakeful relaxation* is what you're looking for, then **Alpha Waves** are what you need.

STEP 3: While listening to your selection, close your eyes and simply enjoy the sound at a comfortable level for about 10 minutes as you prepare your brain for the day.

STEP 4: During your day, whether it's during your lunch break or a period where you just need to clear or refocus your mind, put your headphones on and listen to your selected frequency. Doing so while you're busy in the middle of a task or in need of motivation will be of great service to you as well.

Once more time, for emphasis, be sure your daily dietary needs include foods that help promote brain power.

Overall, there's no one way to make good use of the brain entrainment frequencies outside of simply listening to them. It's best to listen in the morning like a meditation session— as if you were working out at a gym designed for your brain—to help your brain wake up and be best prepared for daily activities. You see, your brain consists of networks of neurons. By entraining your brain like training a muscle on a regular basis, you are opening up more neural pathways and strengthening existing ones, allowing you to think faster and clearer having all these neurons and synapses interconnected.

Also, you should play these binaural beats whenever you're reading or need to concentrate on a work-based project (Gamma Waves), or if you're simply looking to expand you creativity (Alpha Waves**).

**The University of North Carolina (UNC) School of Medicine identified that a low dose of electric current of 10-hertz can enhance alpha brainwave activity and boosts creativity by 7.4% in healthy adults.

DAY 3:

Strengthen Your Connection with Body and Mind

Better Wiring with Writing

Day 3 will incorporate what we've covered thus far plus the addition of another technique, wait for it...writing. *Surprised?* After all, you have been doing it your whole life and maybe even every day.

What does writing do for the brain?

Within the ever-advancing technological landscape of our world, there's been some debate in recent years as to whether or not the teaching of *handwriting* should be altogether abandoned in favor of *typing* in schools. As such, future generations would know nothing of using pen and paper. It's the same way with how *cursive* is no longer taught in most school districts.

In the age of age digital, it would seem that the art of handwriting has become obsolete. However, new studies blow this narrative right out of the water.

Graphologist and handwriting expert Dr. Marc J. Seifer has conducted studies that show how writing with pen (or pencil or quill, etc.) requires more complex brain functions than typing. This is based on how the process of physically writing information down on a piece of paper is a symbiotic act of body and mind. It combines the visual with both the cognitive and the motor skills of the brain, giving both the cerebrum and cerebellum a **good workout**.

In that regard, writing makes the brain work on multiple levels all at once as the visual aspect requires being able to look at the paper, the cognitive revolves around memory (such as the various symbols involved in writing/language along with their coordination and arrangement), and motor skills are needed to do the physical writing.

Exercise: Mindful Mixing and Matching

As with Day 2, you will need to start your brain stimulation, right away, first thing in the morning.

Of course, you will need to eat a breakfast made up of the brain power foods (this should be starting to become fairly routine at this point).

After breakfast, select a frequency track for the day. Take into consideration each one and what its purpose is. So, for example, if you feel like you want more concentration today, you should choose to listen to the one that emits Beta Waves:

- Meditation Version:

www.youtube.com/watch?v=z-tf5Iu5io8

- Raw Version:

www.youtube.com/watch?v=vEHVz5XCmBs

While listening to your selection, try to be mindful of where your thoughts go. In doing so, go ahead and write down, with pen and paper already on hand, what you're thinking about. Make sure to write full sentences and try to get about **ten lines** down. While you're writing, be sure to really give full and clear details about what you're thinking. Throughout this process, make a diligent effort to be as grammatically sound as possible in your writing.

To make the best of and conserve your levels of concentration, today would be a good day to start taking one of the cognition-enhancing infusions. These could include ginseng, Matcha, Gingko tea, or whatever one you prefer. For best results, try to take it between lunchtime and 4:00 P.M.

Throughout your day, be sure to be consistent about using the binaural beat that will help you focus your tasks. Outside of the initial exercise, it's not always necessary to combine the brain entrainment listening with the writing (unless that is the actually task you're focusing on) as your hands might be preoccupied with another task, such as tying something up or lifting boxes.

Relaxing at home, you can use the Alpha Wave frequency to calm your brain down as you prepare for a restful night's sleep. Doing so will help you alleviate stress and prepare your focus for the next day. It might also be helpful to combine some of these "lighter sessions" with a bit of writing just before bedtime. That way, your brain can be alert, and calm itself down in more gradual steps rather than shutting down in a more drastic manner due to fatigue or exhaustion.

DAY 4:

Synchronize Your Left and Right Hemispheres

Molding the Brain Anyway You Like

On **Day 4** you'll start to gain better understanding of how to tap your brain's unfettered potential by having a better grasp on how it functions. That being said, it's commonly believed that all of the functions, both mental and physiological, of the brain are housed within the right and left hemispheres.

Specifically, the **left hemisphere** is what controls logic, analysis, memorizing facts, and the necessary cognitions for abstract concepts such as math and language. The **right hemisphere** is responsible for the more the hands-on components of living such as creativity, imagination, intuition, artistic endeavors, rhythm, feelings, and visualization.

At one point, people believed that you could only ever use one of the hemispheres effectively, leading to the assumption that an individual was either only really good with sciences or only gifted with abilities in the arts.

This outdated way of thinking about the brain and its two halves started to change in 2008 when Robert Epstein, Ph.D. and psychology researcher, published a study in *Creativity Research Journal (Vol. 20, No. 1)* that conveyed some groundbreaking results. His research focused on cognitive development in core areas such as taking in new ideas, broadening knowledge, engaging in challenging tasks, and interacting with stimulating people and places. What he found in his study demonstrated that the brain can shift from one side of the brain to the other. Such a notion about the human mind gives greater insight into how its own faculties help to promote innovation and better problem-solving skills.

Sharper and enhanced thinking across both hemispheres is the aim of the game with this program.

So, begin today by having breakfast utilizing what you can from the brain-boosting foods. (If you were prescribed by a doctor, take your nootropic supplement.)

The next step involves a process of listening to two binaural beats for about ten minutes each.

Exercise 1: Let Problems be Solved

First up is the Gamma frequency:

- Meditation Version:
www.youtube.com/watch?v=clwVxrQ3vFo
- Raw Version:
www.youtube.com/watch?v=axTImghP9Ts

This frequency will stimulate the left side of your brain as the cognitions connected to logic, abstraction, and problem solving become more active.

While listening to this frequency, it's time for your first mental exercise.

Complete the crossword puzzle below to really get the brain juices flowing for the day. As you complete the task, continue listening to the Gamma Waves for a little while longer. This puzzle shouldn't take you any longer than ten minutes, maybe fifteen at the very most.

B	E	S	T	L	O	X
R	A	G	M	C	A	R
S	U	N	N	Y	O	X
B	B	S	L	A	S	T
W	Y	L	Q	D	R	Q
E	O	I	K	T	U	O
P	K	W	R	O	N	G

Instructions:

There are **ten words** in the table above. Some of them can be backwards, upside down, or diagonal. Use the hints below to help you complete this exercise in **less than 15 minutes**:

1. It's a fruit used to make our favorite breakfast drink.

2. When the sun is out, it is said to be...

3. The opposite of walking.

4. A mature person should know the difference between right and...

5. The opposite of in.

6. It is used to write a verb in the infinitive.

7. When you give it your all you give your...

8. It is used to measure a candidate's popularity during the elections.

9. We need it to go to work.

10. Something that never ends.

SOLUTION:

B	E	S	T			
		G		C	A	R
S	U	N	N	Y		
			L	A	S	T
		L			R	
	O			T	U	O
P		W	R	O	N	G

Exercise 2: Let Creativity Flow

After the crossword puzzle, your next task will be to awaken the right side of your brain to activate your creativity and intuition.

For this next exercise, listen to the Beta Wave* frequency for 10 minutes then stop:

- Meditation Version:
www.youtube.com/watch?v=z-tf5Iu5io8
- Raw Version:
www.youtube.com/watch?v=vEHVz5XCmBs

*Why not Alpha Wave this time? You want to be a little more alert than laidback for this exercise, thus the next higher level frequency above Alpha is the Beta Wave frequency.

Then do the following exercise:

Describe the image above. Here's how you will proceed:

1. First, describe what you see. For this, write a maximum of about **100 words.**

2. Next, describe the materials used to create this image. For instance, how is it created by the artists? Was it crafted digitally on a screen, as a drawing on paper, or something else entirely? For this part, write a maximum of **50 words.**

3. Finally, try to express the kinds of emotions/thoughts the image provokes within you. For example, does it remind you of a particular time or place or does it inspire you to travel to far off places? Whatever comes to mind when viewing this image, write about it in a maximum of **200 words.**

During the entire process, continue listening to the Beta Waves all throughout.

Learn to Use Both Sides of Your Brain

Throughout these exercises, you might start to take note of how you can shift gears in your mind to access both sides of your brain as you jump across your own mental landscape. This is exemplified by how one side will have pushed itself to solve a problem while the other does its best to interpret a piece of art immediately afterwards.

As with the previous days, use the binaural beats to help you focus or relax when you need to throughout the day. In doing so, you may find yourself exploring the hidden abilities of your brain as you move towards a state of polyvalence (the capacity for possessing and utilizing flexible intelligence using both hemispheres of the brain).

We are now done for today until tomorrow for **Day 5.**

DAY 5:

Speed Up Your Cognitive Processing Ability

A Faster Mind through Speed Reading

Back in the day, we were all told as young things that reading was the best thing since sliced bread. This was mostly due to the way literacy would help to improve grammatical skills as well as help to strengthen one's imagination (as reading a novel is, after all, a far cry from watching T.V.), to say nothing of the fact that one can't get very far in this world without the ability to read.

On a cognitive level, reading has actually been shown to decrease stress (one of your brain cells' greatest threats in life) due to the way it processes information. Professionals such as Robert S. Wilson at the Rush University Medical Center in Chicago encourages everyone to read more often due to the fact that it can fight the effects of a declining memory.

For Day 5, you will be concentrating on **speed reading** to give your brain a good workout on processing information faster.

Studies have shown that the average person can read about **200** to **400** words per minute. Practicing speed reading can help you to double or triple that number.

Don't know what your reading speed is? Then take the Staples free reading test.

Additionally, you will be able to better grasp the structure and gain a better understanding of the overall bigger picture of what you are reading. These certainly sound like good attributes to have, so let's get started.

Exercise: A Memory Scan

1. Begin your morning with a brain power breakfast. Next, have some Matcha tea or other supplements to get your mind awake and alert.

2. Next, you should pick the binaural beat that is best suited for reading. In this case, it's the Beta Wave frequency as it helps with active concentration and all that jazz. You should begin your session by listening to the track for about two minutes to jumpstart your brain. At that point, you should be active and ready for the reading activity.

3. Read the text below by scanning through it (this will help to stimulate your brain as it is quickly pushed

towards identifying the main points). In the process of scanning the information, follow this methodology:

STEP 1: Read in a linear fashion. This will allow you to scan the content much better and at a faster rate.

STEP 2: Look for titles and subtitles, etc. to get a better idea of what the text is going to be about. This step is an imperative as it will help you to put the pieces together as you progress through the reading.

STEP 3: Scan for bullet points or words in bold. Most of the time, these will represent a summary of ideas or key points within a document.

Throughout the entirety of this process, keep in mind that you should be listening to the Beta Waves.

With these instructions in mind, the task shouldn't take any longer than fifteen minutes.

One of the biggest debates in education these last few years has been about the enforcement of online classes as a tutorial method. People were more used to long distance learning and face to face learning, but online learning has been a new trend that has made a lot of people skeptical, at first.

Taking classes and exams on a computer can be distracting as there are so many other things you can do while you are online. With that said, one question comes to mind; is online teaching as effective as face to face teaching?

We will now try to cover the pros and cons of each teaching method and see how the two compare and how they diverge, so that we can come up with a solid answer to the above question.

Online classes promote more concentration on behalf of the student compared to face to face classes:

In fact, online classes enable the student to isolate him(her) self from noises and any other type of distraction and really concentrate on the class. By taking classes online, you also have access to online resources that will help you have an in-depth knowledge of the subject in study. However, with face to face classes, the lecturer or teacher is like the moderator as you must pay attention to his guidance and explanations of the subject. When you take face to face classes, you have the interpretation of a specialist with the right words, allowing you to understand faster, which is something you may not have with an online class. To help solve this problem, where the student may feel overwhelmed with subjects he does not necessarily understand first hand, online tools such as the one provided by the UMUC like the LEO application helps the student navigate through it, ask questions directly to the lecturer or other students or participate in online conferences. There is also the option to visit the University online library and other learning tools or resources such as the self-evaluation option and course content.

Online classes give more freedom to learn to students:

With online classes, students have the time to do other things like working, pursuing a hobby or going shopping, etc. Something that would be far more difficult with a face to face class, as you will have to report to the class at a requested time frame, which is normally from 8 AM to later for day classes and from 7PM till later for night classes. With an online class you are provided with a weekly program and content to study with an assignment, test or quiz to be submitted by the end of the week. So, students have more time and freedom to read their content, make some more research online if they wish to and then be ready to prepare and write their tests (in whichever format they come) and submit them on time before the deadline, which is normally by the end of the week by midnight.

Upon completion of the reading, with Beta Waves still playing, **write a sentence** on what you think the text is about.

Keep in mind that it may feel like quite a bit of effort trying to scan a document followed by an attempt at deciphering its meaning. As such, you might want to go through the text once more to try to fully comprehend it. Should that be the case, it's not really an issue. It's simply an indication that you might not quite be adjusted to this speed reading technique just yet. Nevertheless, just trust your instinct and write down whatever it is you think the document is about or trying to convey.

Before bedtime (and this is entirely optional), you can double check the material to see what it was about as you read through it at a normal pace this time around. You can even do this while preparing for a restful night sleep by listing to the Alpha Wave frequency.

DAY 6:

Shape Your Brain through Thoughts

Your Mood Affects Your Thinking

Good thinking is basically another term for positive thinking. Those who exude this mentality through their outlook on life find themselves able to solve problems faster and to a greater degree than those who are easily overcome by stress, sadness, or anger.

As with all of the other brain-boosting techniques, this isn't just something we're making up out of thin air. Really, this is legit.

In fact, in 1890, William James, an American Philosopher and Psychologist, had come to the conclusion that our very thoughts could drastically alter the structure and functions of our brains. This theory holds that the brain has the capacity to adapt easily on the basis that it is a dynamic organ, one whose magnitude we're only starting to fully understand.

In recent years, this theory surrounding good thinking has risen in popularity among psychologists and other members of the scientific community. Many of them have encouraged people to engage in positive thinking under all circumstances, even those of extreme duress. This has resulted in less stress and depression with an increase in hope in the subjects implanting the good thinking technique.

As such, these individuals had an improved problem-solving skill set and, by extension, more active and regenerated brain cells (many of which, as previously mentioned, can be destroyed by stress).

Exercise: No Problems at All

So, what's the most effective way to implement good thinking to optimize your brain functions early in the morning and throughout the rest of your day?

When you first crawl out of bed, begin with this "ritual" before doing anything else:

STEP 1: Tell yourself "It's a new day with new challenges, and I have to look and feel my very best."

STEP 2: Tell yourself "I will use my morning routine before I head off for the day as the jumpstart point to the rest of what I wish to accomplish." With this step, you will be pushing yourself to better prepare for the day. Try to focus, and think positive thoughts about the tasks ahead of you for the day.

STEP 3: Tell yourself "Whatever happens outside of this house, I will face it all with optimism and determination."

STEP 4: Tell yourself "Nothing can ever be perfect, but perfection can be found in problem solving and not losing control of myself during the day."

Since today's goals are focused on problem solving, give the Gamma Wave frequency a listen for ten minutes before leaving for day. This way, your focus and positive affirmation can embed themselves into your mind more easily.

Afterwards, you should be good to go. Eat your brain-empowering breakfast and prepare yourself for the day (morning routines, taking a shower, getting dressed, etc.) with a sense of motivation and positively-charged brain!

Throughout the day, when you're feeling tired or sluggish, you can repeat these words to yourself:

- "The day is not over yet, but I still need it give it my very best."

- "I have a great routine that I will repeat tomorrow, so I shouldn't deviate from its purpose, which is to prepare myself to give my very best."

- "I can still face whatever challenges come my way before the day ends."

- "Nothing can ever be perfect, but perfection can be found in problem solving and not losing control of myself during the day."

Once again, listen to the Gamma Wave frequency as you allow these affirmations to settle into your subconscious.

DAY 7:

Exercise Your Brain

It's Game Time!

You made it all the way to **Day 7**! For this final day of your seven-day brain power training, we've saved the very best for last!

Today, you will be doing some **mind exercise** games. These are said to be an excellent way to fight off the effects of Alzheimer's.

In a clinical study, Glenn Smith, Ph.D. and neuropsychologist at the Mayo Clinic, analyzed the role of mind exercises with regard to the brain and concluded that they can be beneficial. This is based on how the persistence in mind exercises are the most effective at maintaining a healthy brain.

But, there's no reason to wait until you start getting older when you can start sharpening your cognitions today by jumping on exercising your mind on a regular basis.

For Day 7 you will:

1. Have your brain-boosting breakfast along with some Matcha, or another supplement of your choosing, for focus.

2. Then, before turning on your tablet or PC or even opening up reading material from a newspaper, magazine, etc., try these two morning mind exercises. To make things go more smoothly, give the Theta

Wave frequency a quick listen to clear your mind before you begin work:

- Meditation Version:

www.youtube.com/watch?v=CreU9g302yU

- Raw Version:

www.youtube.com/watch?v=66tq9xji0xA

Morning Exercise 1: Words Identification

Complete the words in the table below <u>horizontally</u> to reveal the keyword in the highlighted boxes. Use the following clues to solve the puzzle:

1	B	O			
2		R		C	A
3	S				
4	H		B		T
5			D		

<u>ROW 1</u>: It describes an upward leaping motion.

<u>ROW 2</u>: The female version of the name Eric.

<u>ROW 3</u>: It's a country situated on the Iberian Peninsula.

<u>ROW 4</u>: It's something that you develop through time and can make part of your routine.

<u>ROW 5</u>: Also known as part of Ancient Nubia.

SOLUTION:

B	O	U	N	D
E	**R**	I	C	A
S	P	A	I	N
H	A	B	I	T
S	U	D	A	N

Morning Exercise 2: Numerical Solutions

Complete these math problems without using a calculator:

333 x 2+ 10,000 = ?

555 + 5 x 5 x 2 = ?

2 x 2 x 2 + 2 + 2 - 2 = ?

1/3 +30 x 2 = ?

100 x 100 x 100 + 30 = ?

Try to solve these problems as fast as you can, within the scope of about five minutes.

SOLUTIONS:

333 x 2 + 10,000 = 10,666

555 + 5 x 5 x 2 = 605

2 x 2 x 2 + 2 + 2 − 2 = 10

1/3 + 30 x 2 = 60.33 (or 181/3)

100 x 100 x 100 + 30 = 1,000,030

Midday Exercise: Text Interpretation

At around midday, play the Gamma Wave frequency:

- Meditation Version:

www.youtube.com/watch?v=clwVxrQ3vFo

- Raw Version:

www.youtube.com/watch?v=axTImghP9Ts

As you listen, take about five minutes to scan through the text below before answering the questions that follow (try not to look at the material as you answer the questions):

The Museum specializes in artifacts recovered in the Bay of Naples during the last 2 centuries. Once called the Bourbon Museum, its collection of artifacts is spectacular and speaks for itself and demonstrate just why Rome and Greece were great civilizations.

They were great when they ruled the known world, and when they were no longer there, humanity's quest for "reason" and "beauty" had to go back to "dig out " these 2 civilizations, come out of the dark ages and find enough inspiration to mold the world as it is today.

But, we tend to forget about the great ones that were not so lucky. Like Pompeii that was dramatically whipped in 79 A.D by the eruption of Mount Vesuvius (a volcano near Naples). Many artifacts still intact were recovered on the bay of Naples and these artifacts are still intact, today.

We have visited one of the rooms of the Archeological Museum of Napoli online to better stress that assertion. Greece and Rome count amongst the greatest civilizations ever known and during their many centuries of conquests and knowledge, many who contributed to their "grandeur" were lost and are only know to us today, thanks to the artifacts discovered almost 2000 years after they disappeared.

This exercise should go by pretty fast. For each answer, write down whatever comes to mind and you can double check your answers in the text later (if you choose to).

- What civilization is brought up in the text?

- What historical period is mentioned in the text?

- What dramatic event occurred that erased an entire region?

- What make the civilizations mentioned in the text so great?

Nighttime Exercise: Imagery Differentiation

Before going to bed, do this one last mind game below (this time, use the Theta Wave frequency):

The task is simple, just find the errors...

Observe the **picture below** (have a brief five minute look at the picture and memorize it):

Compare it to **this second image** and find the *differences between the two*:

Keep in mind that, even though this is Day 7, you should still be treating your brain right by eating healthy brain-fuel foods as well as engaging in the other techniques from the previous days. It's important to remember that, whether you're working or resting today, mind exercises are an essential for keeping your brain active and healthy for a long time to come.

As you go to bed, you should end this week by making sure you get a restful and rejuvenating night's sleep. To do this (and this might become part of your weekly ritual for Day 7) play the Delta Wave frequency as you fall asleep:

- Meditation Version:

www.youtube.com/watch?v=txQ6t4yPIM0

- Raw Version:

www.youtube.com/watch?v=JnhFsHyeeNQ

Doing so will help you to have deep and dreamless sleep so that your brain can relax like a day at the spa after a week of hard work.

SOLUTION:

Schedule Regular Reboots to Boost

It's good to disconnect and go "screen-less" sometimes. In other words, it's for the best that you don't allow technology to take over your brain's role. Because it is kind of a miracle of existence, housing consciousness, memories, thoughts, and dreams, the brain should never be replaced by a machine. Like any part of the body, you have to care for and make the most of it no matter what.

That being said, here's a brief list of guidelines you can integrate into your lifestyle/routine from here on in:

1. Always try to find a balance between technology use and good habits. Some of the new practices you should acquire this week, such as putting words on paper on a more regular basis, can never be replaced by a digital device. This is not only a matter of the differences between analog and digital, but also because of the way

these types of activities stimulate your brain as they help make you more alert and smarter.

2. Always eat foods that promote a healthy and active brain. Healthy meals are essential here, especially those that can give natural energy.

3. Make good use of natural supplements, as opposed to those that are overloaded with chemicals. Both can give you the same effect, but the non-organic ones often lead to a dependency that will ultimately cause the opposite of what you need for an empowered brain. So, always remember that healthy infusion teas such as Matcha or Gingko Biloba (along with other natural brain stimulants) are the ideal way to go and that you don't have to take them all the time like medications.

4. Incorporate the techniques from this week as a part of your routine from now on. This means getting up about fifteen to twenty minutes earlier to start implementing some of the strategies of this week.

DAY 1: Apply the **clear thinking** method.

DAY2: Start using the **binaural beats.**

DAY 3: Throw some **writing** into the mix (you can even go out and get a journal if you want).

DAY 4: Start to use both sides of your brain for **cerebral synchronization utilization.**

DAY 5: Combine brain entrainment with **speed reading.**

DAY 6: Practice problem solving through **good thinking** *aka* positive **thinking.**

DAY 7: is a mix of all of these along with **mind exercises.**

After this week, the biggest test will be to see if you can continue using these techniques, allowing them to build off each other, every day from here on in. Remember, try not get too discouraged and that you can do this!

5. Allow your body to relax and rest. Getting about seven to eight hours of sleep is just what your brain needs to reboot itself and alleviate the stresses that often put a strain on it. If you can, try to take naps throughout your day, as this is an effective way to revitalize your mind and make it function properly.

Overall, every week from now should be about rebooting and exercising your brain. This seven-day brain power challenge isn't about just using your brain as some kind of fancy or sophisticated tool designed simply to serve you. Instead, the entire point of all of this is to promote a healthy brain by inserting good and healthy habits into your daily routines. However, that's not all—the dangers of Dementia, Alzheimer's, the destruction of brain cells, and other forms of mental degradation should not be taken lightly. By making brain training a part of your life, you can reduce your risk of falling victim to any of these by keeping your brain healthier for longer.

Challenge Complete:

Brain Empowered

When in tip-top shape, our brains can make us the envy of those around us by always exhibiting the best ideas, coming across as highly articulate, as well as appearing as sharp as a tack.

But, as mentioned before, the gifts of a beautiful mind are things that we are susceptible to losing just like our ridiculously good looks. The primary cause is the natural course of aging, but that doesn't mean we can't do something about it the meantime.

Through a healthy and active lifestyle that promotes brain empowerment, one can slow the effects of mental degradation. Sometimes we forget or neglect to do things that can help us, such as getting a full night's sleep or eating our vegetables, both good things (among many others) that will help our brains in the long run.

Like any muscle, the brain needs stimulation and exercise, lest it become a sloth. Helping our brains run better is all based around gaining an understanding of how it functions. What your brain really needs is no more than a change in how you live your life. All it takes is about twenty minutes from your morning and little things throughout the day to jumpstart it and keep it going.

If you implement these changes and techniques into your lifestyle and are diligent enough to keep them up, you will start to feel better and see improvements in your cognitive skills.

Your brain is a treasure. It is the tool of your biology that allows reality itself to reveal itself to you and allow you take that reality in. So take some time every day to stimulate and better persevere its abilities. And remember—you totally got this!

<u>Your Feedback:</u>

Was Your Challenge Accomplished?

Congratulations on completing all your challenges! You should be proud of yourself for making it this far. For that, give yourself a big pat on the back! :)

Now, we have a huge favor that we would like to ask you. We want to know: have you accomplished the goal you established when you began this trial?

No two people are the same, so results will always vary.

If you have seen the results you wanted, give yourself another pat on the back, and please kindly share your testimonial wherever you purchased this book. If you let us know about it, we have a small free gift to offer you as a token of our appreciation.

However, if you aren't satisfied in any way, we urge you to please contact us directly to let us know what could have been different to help you achieve better results. We want to know if there is any way we can further help you.

Plus we are very easy to get a hold of online!

Official Website:
http://www.ChallengeSelf.com

Social Media:
https://www.facebook.com/ChallengeSelf
https://twitter.com/MyChallengeSelf
https://plus.google.com/+Challengeself

"YOU" are our main priority, and we're all here for you!

Take care! And always challenge yourself!